CHAPTER 1

ARRIVAL OF THE DRAGON

2

6

8

WHO WAS BRUCE LEE?

THE BIG BOSS

CHINESE CONNECTION

WAY OF THE DRAGON

EVEN THOUGH HE ONLY MADE FIVE MOVIES AS AN ADULT, HE BECAME A LEGEND.

ENTER THE DRAGON

GAME OF DEATH

HE WAS A STUDENT.

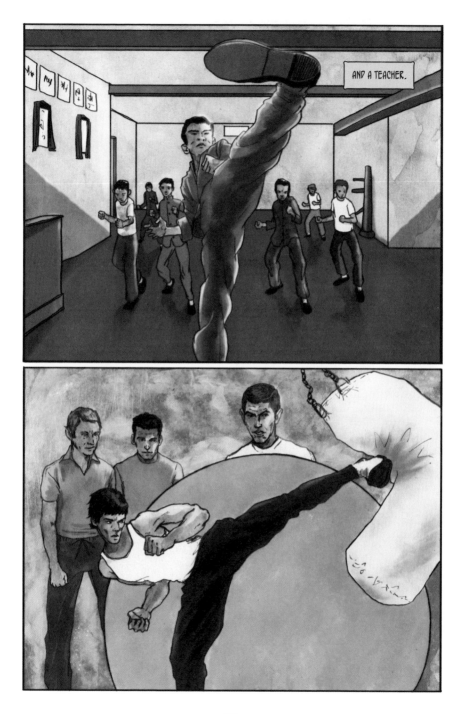

13

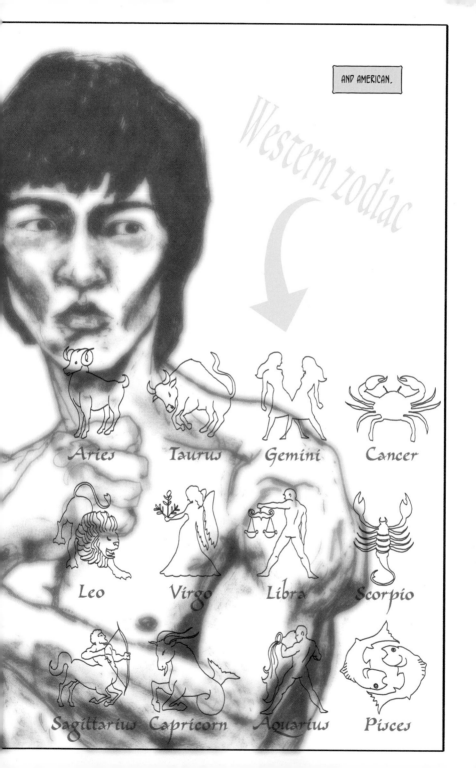

Western zodiac

Aries   Taurus   Gemini   Cancer

Leo   Virgo   Libra   Scorpio

Sagittarius   Capricorn   Aquarius   Pisces

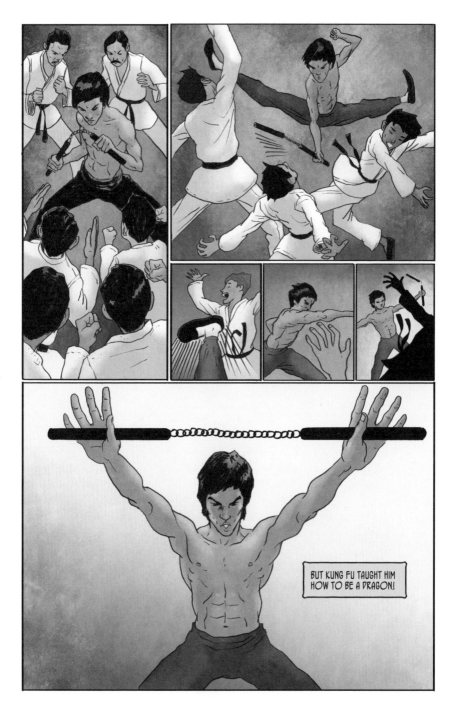

BUT KUNG FU TAUGHT HIM HOW TO BE A DRAGON!

"If you love life, don't waste time, for time is what life is made of."

—Bruce Lee

THE MYSTICAL REALM OF
THE CHINESE ZODIAC.

FEBRUARY 8, 1940
(CHINESE NEW YEAR)

EVERY YEAR . . .

NOVEMBER 1940

SAN FRANCISCO, CALIFORNIA, USA

GRACE HO LOVED TWO THINGS MOST IN LIFE: HER FAMILY AND READING.

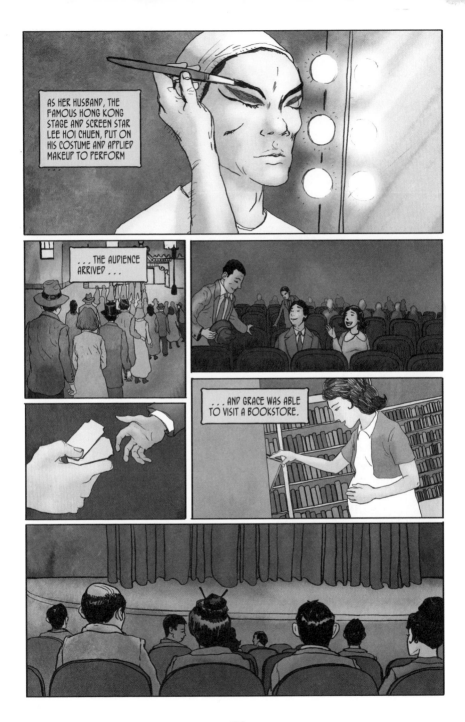

AS HER HUSBAND, THE FAMOUS HONG KONG STAGE AND SCREEN STAR LEE HOI CHUEN, PUT ON HIS COSTUME AND APPLIED MAKEUP TO PERFORM . . .

. . . THE AUDIENCE ARRIVED . . .

. . . AND GRACE WAS ABLE TO VISIT A BOOKSTORE.

AMERICAN AUDIENCES WERE WOWED WITH HIS DYNAMIC PERFORMANCE IN THE CANTONESE OPERA.

AND WHILE HER HUSBAND PERFORMED IN FRONT OF A PACKED HOUSE--

--SHE WAS ABLE TO RELAX IN HIS DRESSING ROOM WITH A NEW BOOK--

--AND SHARE IT WITH THEIR UNBORN CHILD.

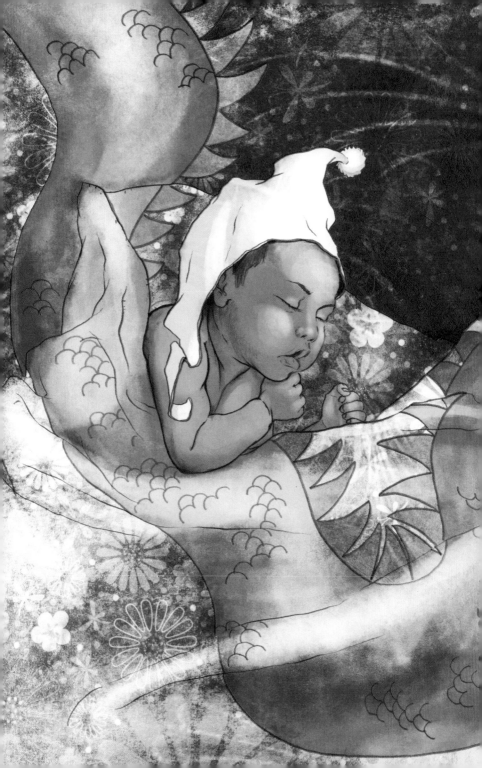

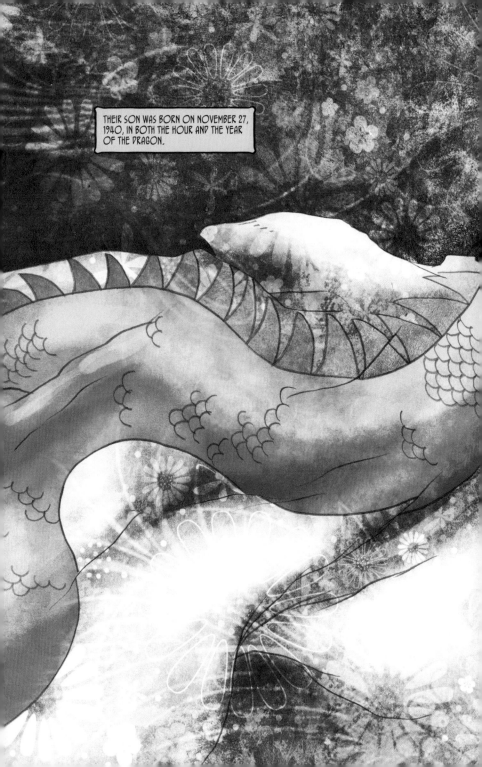

THEIR SON WAS BORN ON NOVEMBER 27, 1940, IN BOTH THE HOUR AND THE YEAR OF THE DRAGON.

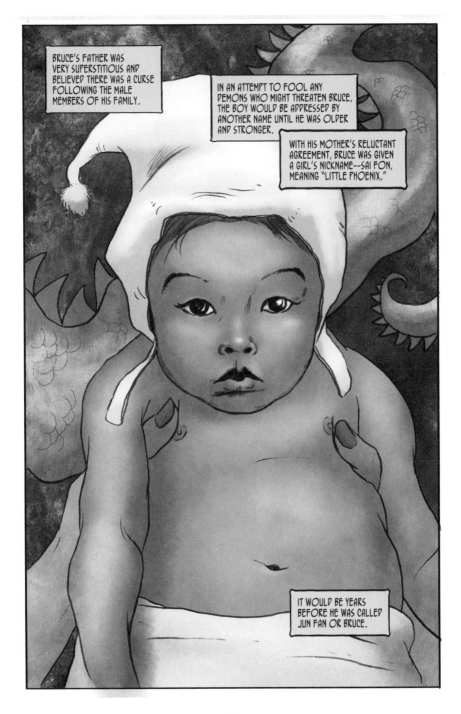

BRUCE'S FATHER WAS VERY SUPERSTITIOUS AND BELIEVED THERE WAS A CURSE FOLLOWING THE MALE MEMBERS OF HIS FAMILY.

IN AN ATTEMPT TO FOOL ANY DEMONS WHO MIGHT THREATEN BRUCE, THE BOY WOULD BE ADDRESSED BY ANOTHER NAME UNTIL HE WAS OLDER AND STRONGER.

WITH HIS MOTHER'S RELUCTANT AGREEMENT, BRUCE WAS GIVEN A GIRL'S NICKNAME--SAI FON, MEANING "LITTLE PHOENIX."

IT WOULD BE YEARS BEFORE HE WAS CALLED JUN FAN OR BRUCE.

AFTER SEVERAL MORE MONTHS OF WORK IN THE UNITED STATES, INCLUDING THE INFANT'S FIRST APPEARANCE IN A MOVIE, THE LEES BOARDED A SHIP AND BEGAN THE JOURNEY HOME TO HONG KONG.

BRUCE WAS ABOUT TO MEET HIS FAMILY!

UNFORTUNATELY, HE BECAME ILL ON THE LONG TRIP. DESPITE CONSTANT LOVING CARE FROM HIS PARENTS, HE WOULD REMAIN IN HIS WEAKENED CONDITION FOR MONTHS.

WHEN THEY ARRIVED IN HONG KONG, MR. AND MRS. LEE WERE OPTIMISTIC ABOUT THEIR SON'S HEALTH, KNOWING THERE WOULD SOON BE OTHERS TO SHARE THEIR LOVE DURING HIS RECUPERATION.

THE LEE RESIDENCE CONSISTED OF BRUCE'S SISTERS, PHOEBE AND AGNES; HIS BROTHER, PETER;

TWO CATS; THREE DOGS; TWO BIRDS; TWO FISH;

MR. LEE'S SISTER-IN-LAW (WHOSE HUSBAND, MR. LEE'S BROTHER, HAD PASSED AWAY);

HER FIVE CHILDREN;

FROM TIME TO TIME MR. LEE'S MOTHER;

THREE HOUSEHOLD STAFF MEMBERS;

WU NGAN, THE SON OF THE COOK;

AND A VARIETY OF COUSINS AND RELATIVES VISITING ON A REGULAR BASIS,

WHICH BROUGHT THE TOTAL NUMBER OF PEOPLE USUALLY LIVING IN THE HOUSE TO TWENTY OR MORE!

THE LINE FOR THE *ONE* BATHROOM EVERY MORNING WAS QUITE COMPETITIVE.

43

45

CHAPTER 2

BLACK CHRISTMAS

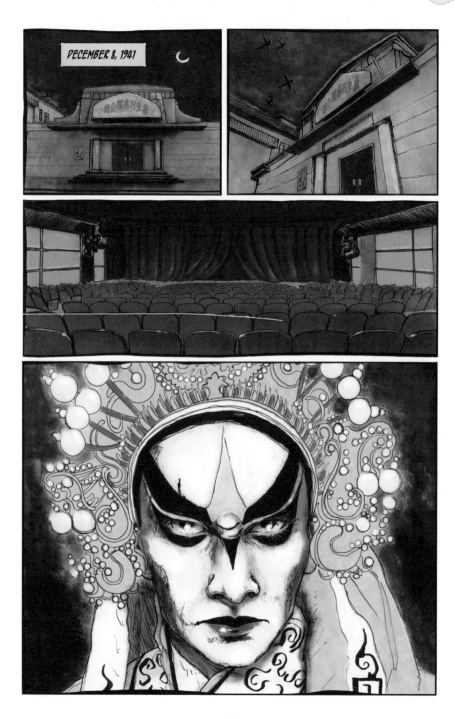

SINCE 1842, HONG KONG HAD BEEN A BRITISH COLONY, AND THUS WAS DEFENDED BY A COMBINATION OF OUTSIDE FORCES IN CONJUNCTION WITH ITS OWN.

HOURS AFTER JAPAN BOMBED THE US NAVAL BASE AT PEARL HARBOR, THEY ALSO ATTACKED HONG KONG. IT WAS AN EXPANSION OF THEIR EFFORTS TO CONTROL ASIAN TERRITORIES THAT HAD BEGUN YEARS BEFORE IN MAINLAND CHINA.

ON DECEMBER 25, 1941, AFTER SEVENTEEN DAYS OF ATTACKS, THE INVADING FORCES OVERWHELMED THE LOCAL, BRITISH, CANADIAN, AND INDIAN TROOPS, FORCING THE HONG KONG GOVERNMENT TO SURRENDER TO IMPERIAL JAPAN.

OCCUPYING FORCES WENT ABOUT RENAMING BUSINESSES AND STREETS WITH JAPANESE NAMES. EVENTUALLY, BOOKS AND TEXTBOOKS WOULD BE CONVERTED AS WELL.

JAPANESE BECAME MANDATORILY TAUGHT IN SCHOOL . . .

. . . AND LEARNING IT WAS ENFORCED BY THE THREAT OF PHYSICAL PUNISHMENT.

THE HONG KONG DOLLAR WAS OUTLAWED AND REPLACED BY THE JAPANESE MILITARY YEN. AT FIRST, THE EXCHANGE RATE WAS TWO HONG KONG DOLLARS TO ONE YEN, BUT THEN IT WAS SHIFTED TO FOUR HONG KONG DOLLARS TO ONE YEN.

AS A RESULT, ALL CITIZENS OF HONG KONG INSTANTLY SAW THEIR WEALTH SHRINK TO HALF, AND THEN MONTHS LATER, TO HALF YET AGAIN.

THE UNEMPLOYED WERE DEPORTED TO CHINA--

--WHICH WAS STILL SUFFERING TERRIBLY FROM ITS LONG WAR (THE SECOND SINO-JAPANESE WAR AND THE NANJING MASSACRE) WITH JAPAN.

AS THE JAPANESE ESTABLISHED THEIR GOVERNMENT, ROUGHLY SEVEN THOUSAND BRITISH SOLDIERS AND CIVILIANS WERE KEPT IN PRISONER OF WAR CAMPS, WHERE MALNUTRITION WAS RAMPANT.

OUTSIDE OF THE P.O.W. CAMPS, FOOD WAS RATIONED TO THE CITIZENS IN SMALL, INADEQUATE QUANTITIES. HOSPITALS WERE GOVERNED BY THE JAPANESE AND FORCED TO DECREASE THE SERVICES THEY PROVIDED. SICKNESS AND STARVATION INCREASED.

STILL AFRAID, MR. LEE BEGAN SPEAKING ON BEHALF OF THE JAPANESE.

WITH CHINA PARTLY FALLEN AND EUROPE SOON TO FOLLOW, WE CAN GO ALONG AND PROSPER . . .

. . . OR RESIST AND LOSE EVERYTHING. ULTIMATELY, THIS WILL BE . . . GOOD FOR US.

HIS ROLE, HOWEVER MINOR, IN HELPING THE JAPANESE LEFT HIM FEELING GUILT-RIDDEN, AS IF HE HAD BETRAYED HIS CULTURE TO PROTECT THOSE HE HELD MOST DEAR.

OTHERS FELT NO SUCH PANGS OF GUILT AND WERE WILLING TO HELP THE JAPANESE AS AN OPPORTUNITY TO GAIN A FORM OF POWER THEY'D NEVER HAD BEFORE.

WHILE MR. LEE AND OTHERS IN SIMILAR POSITIONS SUFFERED IN THEIR WAYS, UNDER JAPANESE RULE, THOUSANDS OF OTHER MEN WERE IMPRISONED, DEPORTED, OR EVEN EXECUTED.

MEANWHILE, IT WAS REPORTED THAT THOUSANDS OF WOMEN WERE ASSAULTED BY THE JAPANESE WITHIN THE FIRST MONTH OF THE OCCUPATION.

CHILDREN, OF COURSE, DIDN'T ESCAPE HARM EITHER.

THEY OFTEN WERE WITNESS TO THE VIOLENCE AND HUMILIATION THAT THE ADULTS SUFFERED, OR, SADLY, SUFFERED THOSE THINGS THEMSELVES.

ALONG WITH PHYSICAL ABUSE WAS THE HUMILIATING FEELING OF COOPERATING TO AVOID BEING IMPRISONED OR KILLED.

REMAINING BUSINESSES HAD TO CONFORM TO JAPANESE RULES OR FACE HARSH CONSEQUENCES.

MUCH BETTER NOW, WOULDN'T YOU AGREE?

YES . . . OF COURSE.

MR. LEE'S "COOPERATION" ALLOWED HIM AND HIS FAMILY THE OPPORTUNITY TO RETURN TO SOMETHING RESEMBLING A NORMAL LIFE.

TIME PASSED.

AND WHILE BRUCE AND HIS FAMILY REMAINED SAFE...

...THEIR PROXIMITY TO ONE OF THE MILITARY ENCAMPMENT FACILITIES--RIGHT ACROSS THE STREET--HAUNTED HIM.

FIVE-YEAR-OLD BRUCE WAS ALWAYS AFRAID HIS PARENTS WOULD BE TAKEN AWAY.

WALKING BY EVERY DAY WAS A CONSTANT REMINDER OF THE DANGERS TO EVERYONE.

AND THE MEN IN UNIFORM WERE THE STUFF OF ANGER AND NIGHTMARES.

ON AUGUST 6, 1945, THE UNITED STATES DROPPED AN ATOMIC BOMB ON HIROSHIMA, JAPAN.

THREE DAYS LATER, ANOTHER BOMB WAS DROPPED ON NAGASAKI.

THE JAPANESE SURRENDERED, AND WORLD WAR II ENDED.

JAPANESE WAR CRIMINALS HAD TO FACE SENTENCING.

MEANWHILE, PRISONERS OF WAR WERE SET FREE AT LAST.

AMONG THEM WAS FRANKLIN GIMSON, WHO WAS THE HIGHEST-RANKING BRITISH OFFICIAL IN THE PRISON.

TEMPORARILY, HE ASSUMED CONTROL OF HONG KONG, AS IT HAD BEEN A BRITISH COLONY PRIOR TO THE JAPANESE INVADING.

AS PEOPLE CELEBRATED THE END OF THE WAR AND ALL THE RELIEF AND JOY IT BROUGHT, THERE WERE THOSE WHOSE WOUNDS AND ANGER RAN DEEP. ANGER AGAINST THE JAPANESE, AGAINST THE INJUSTICES IN GENERAL, AND AGAINST THOSE WHO SOME SAW AS COLLABORATORS. THOSE SEEDS WERE PLANTED.

CHAPTER 3

A RETURN TO LIFE

THAT EVENING, THE HOUSEHOLD CELEBRATED MR. LEE'S RETURN TO WORK.

OR, AT LEAST, THE ADULTS DID.

HEY, THAT'S REALLY GOOD, BRUCE!

THAT EVENING.

MOMMY, ACTING WILL BE A LOT OF FUN!

I KNOW. BUT SCHOOL BEGINS TOMORROW AT LONG LAST. IT HAS TAKEN OUR COUNTRY A BIT OF TIME TO RECOVER FROM THE DAMAGE DONE BY THE JAPANESE.

AND SCHOOL WILL BE THE MOST IMPORTANT THING.

CAN I GO IN THE AFTERNOONS? AFTER SCHOOL?

HMM.

OKAY. WE CAN TRY THAT.

THANKS, MOMMY!!

AS IT TURNED OUT, ACTING WAS A NATURAL FIT FOR SIX-YEAR-OLD BRUCE. HE WOULD GO ON TO MAKE TWENTY FILMS THROUGHOUT HIS CHILDHOOD.

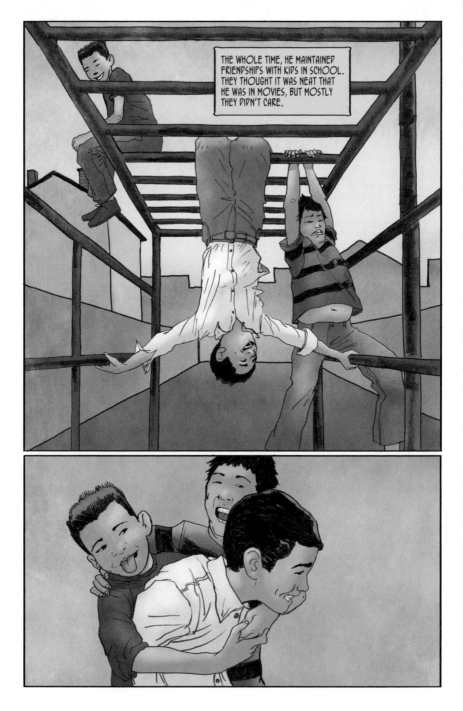

THE WHOLE TIME, HE MAINTAINED FRIENDSHIPS WITH KIDS IN SCHOOL. THEY THOUGHT IT WAS NEAT THAT HE WAS IN MOVIES, BUT MOSTLY THEY DIDN'T CARE.

CHAPTER 4

TROUBLE FOR THE DRAGON

IN 1949, THINGS GOT WORSE IN THE STREETS AS COMMUNISM OVERTOOK CHINA.

THOUSANDS OF REFUGEES FLED. MANY OF THEM CAME TO HONG KONG, SEEKING A NEW BEGINNING.

OH BOY, DO I WANT A CANDY BAR!

ARE THEY OVER THERE?

TENSIONS BETWEEN RACES AND CLASSES GREW. DESPITE THE MULTICULTURALISM IN HONG KONG, PREJUDICES RAN DEEP.

I JUST WANT THIS.

I'M SAVING MY MONEY FOR A--

79

83

WEEKS LATER.

BRUCE CONTINUED TO ACT IN MOVIES AND LOVED MEMORIZING HIS LINES.

HE WAS ALSO A VORACIOUS READER--

--AND COULD OFTEN BE FOUND DEEPLY IMMERSED IN A BOOK.

BUT WHEN IT CAME TO SCHOOL, BRUCE HAD A HARD TIME STAYING INTERESTED.

NOBODY'S PARENTS TOOK THE NEWS WELL.

BRUCE TRIED TO EXPLAIN WHAT HAPPENED . . .

. . . BUT WITH GROWING TROUBLES AT SCHOOL, THEY DIDN'T WANT TO HEAR HIS EXCUSES.

IT UPSET HIM THAT HIS PARENTS DIDN'T BELIEVE HIM.

HIS SIBLINGS WERE PRETTY GOOD ABOUT IT, THOUGH.

WE BELIEVE YOU!

WU NGAN, ON THE OTHER HAND . . .

CAN I HAVE YOUR DOG WHEN YOU WIND UP IN THE ELECTRIC CHAIR?

MISCHIEF WAS THE NEW NORM.

BRUCE'S PERFORMANCE IN SCHOOL REACHED NEW LOWS.

LYING WAS BECOMING EASIER. HE WAS AN ACTOR, AFTER ALL.

I COLLIDED WITH SOMEONE PLAYING BALL IN RECESS. IT'S FINE.

BRUCE WASN'T QUITE HIMSELF, BUT HE DIDN'T SEEM TO REALIZE IT.

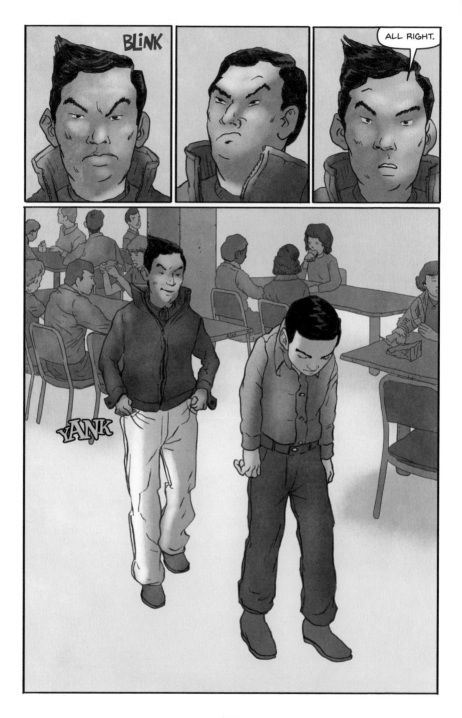

110

THAT NIGHT, STILL PANTLESS, HE DIDN'T KNOW WHAT TO DO. WHEN HIS PANIC GREW, HE EVENTUALLY BEGAN TO SCREAM.

?

HEY, GUYS!

SO WHAT WERE WE TALKING ABOUT AGAIN?

MEANWHILE, CHAN'S PARENTS WERE GREATLY WORRIED. THE POLICE WERE CALLED AND BEGAN THEIR SEARCH AT THE SCHOOL.

WHEN CHAN WAS FOUND, BRUCE WAS IN A LOT OF TROUBLE. HE STILL HAD PLENTY TO LEARN ABOUT RIGHT AND WRONG.

CHAPTER 5

FALL OF THE DRAGON

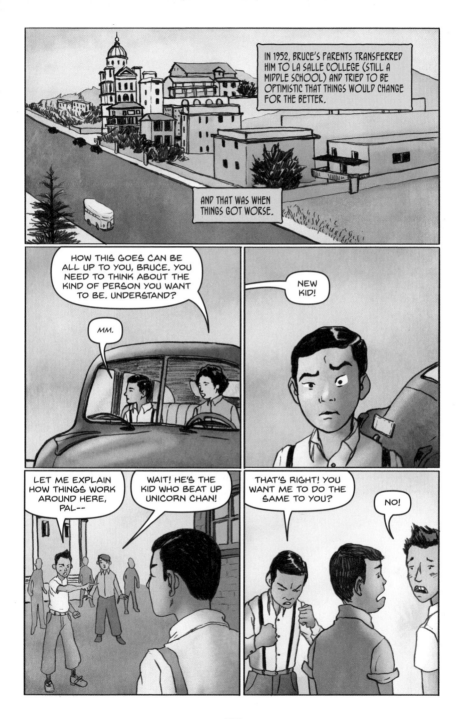

IN 1952, BRUCE'S PARENTS TRANSFERRED HIM TO LA SALLE COLLEGE (STILL A MIDDLE SCHOOL) AND TRIED TO BE OPTIMISTIC THAT THINGS WOULD CHANGE FOR THE BETTER.

AND THAT WAS WHEN THINGS GOT WORSE.

HOW THIS GOES CAN BE ALL UP TO YOU, BRUCE. YOU NEED TO THINK ABOUT THE KIND OF PERSON YOU WANT TO BE. UNDERSTAND?

MM.

NEW KID!

LET ME EXPLAIN HOW THINGS WORK AROUND HERE, PAL--

WAIT! HE'S THE KID WHO BEAT UP UNICORN CHAN!

THAT'S RIGHT! YOU WANT ME TO DO THE SAME TO YOU?

NO!

DESPITE THE EFFORTS OF HIS TEACHER AND PARENTS, BRUCE STILL MANAGED TO FIND CHAOS. THE TIGERS OF JUNCTION STREET MADE TROUBLE, AND FOUND TROUBLE.

GOOD THING US BRITS ARE HERE, OR YOU _____S WOULD ALL BE LIVING LIKE ANIMALS!

I'LL SHOW YOU AN ANIMAL!

RETURNING HOME BY WAY OF THE POLICE AGAIN AND AGAIN FOR FIGHTING IN THE STREETS, BRUCE BEGAN TO BEG HIS PARENTS TO LET HIM LEARN KUNG FU.

NO!

MR. LEE HAD PRACTICED TAI CHI (A MORE INTERNAL, SLOW-MOVING ART) FOR A LONG TIME. WHILE IT CAN BE USED FOR FIGHTING, IT TAKES MANY YEARS TO ATTAIN THE SKILLS NEEDED FOR IT TO BE USED IN SELF-DEFENSE.

CAN I LEARN TAI CHI, AT LEAST?

NO!

WHY NOT? I'M GOING TO GET KILLED OUT THERE AND IT WILL BE YOUR FAULT!

HOW IS THAT SO? SIMPLY AVOID THESE FIGHTS, BRUCE. ATTEND SCHOOL AND RETURN HOME. PLENTY OF PEOPLE GET THROUGH THE DAY WITHOUT FIGHTING OR HAVING THE POLICE TAKE THEM HOME. NOT FIGHTING WILL MAKE YOU WORTHY OF LEARNING HOW TO.

LATER THAT NIGHT.

TWO WEEKS LATER.

BRUCE CONTINUED TO ACT IN A VARIETY OF ROLES IN NUMEROUS MOVIES.

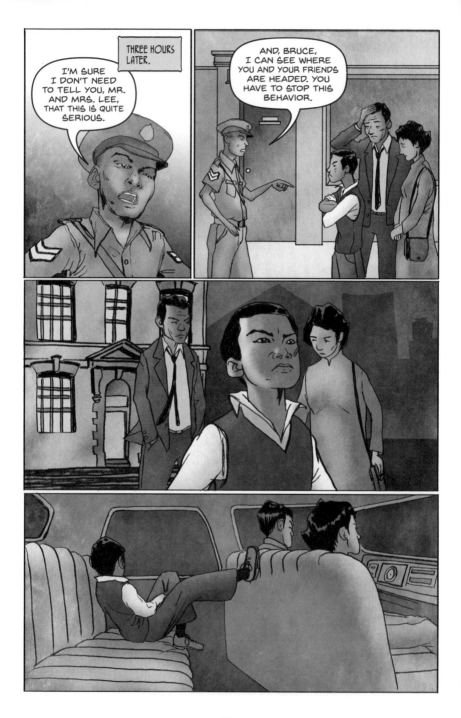

126

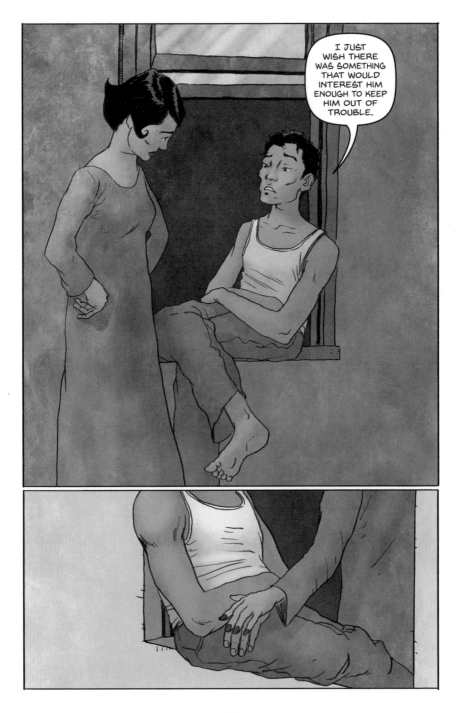

CHAPTER 6

YIP MAN

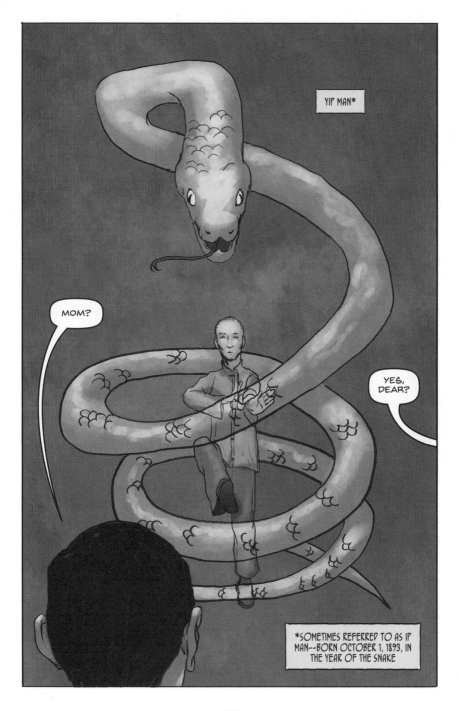

THE NEXT MORNING.

WAKE UP, KIDS! BREAKFAST!

OUCH!

OWOWOW OWOWOW

Tug

I CAN'T REACH ANY OF IT.

OWOWOWOWOW OWOWOWOWOW OWOWOWOWOW OWOWOW

REGARDLESS OF THE PAIN, BRUCE KEPT HIS WORD AND RETURNED IMMEDIATELY AFTER SCHOOL THE NEXT DAY.

WERE THERE THIS MANY STAIRS YESTERDAY?

OWOWOW OWOWOW

YOUNG MASTER BRUCE! GOOD TO SEE YOU TODAY. WERE YOU SORE AFTER YESTERDAY?

HMM? SORE? NO, MASTER.

EXCELLENT! CLASS BEGINS AT FIVE, BUT IN THE MEANTIME, PRACTICE WHAT YOU LEARNED. I WILL COME AROUND.

TODAY WE WILL BE WORKING ON CHI SAO.* FOR BRUCE'S BENEFIT, I WILL REVIEW THE BASICS OF THIS FUNDAMENTAL TECHNIQUE, WHICH IS AT THE CORE OF ALL OF WING CHUN.

*OFTEN REFERRED TO AS "STICKY HANDS"

WHEN PRACTICING CHI SAO, YOU AND YOUR PARTNER ARE ALWAYS PHYSICALLY TOUCHING SO YOU HAVE A CONSTANT FEELING OF ENGAGEMENT . . .

. . . AN EBB AND FLOW TO YOUR MOVEMENT.

THERE ARE THREE STAGES OF CHI SAO TRAINING.

NUMBER ONE: YOU AND YOUR PARTNER BLOCK AND COUNTERSTRIKE USING PREDETERMINED MOVES.

AFTER MUCH TIME TRAINING IN THAT MANNER, YOU MOVE ON TO THE SECOND STAGE OF CHI SAO.

NUMBER TWO: BLOCKING AND COUNTERING EACH OTHER USING ONLY RANDOM MOVES.

IN BOTH OF THESE STAGES OF TRAINING, YOU MUST LEARN TO REMAIN RELAXED, BUT READY--GRACEFUL AND AT EASE, YET ON THE BRINK OF POWER.

ONLY WHEN YOU HAVE BECOME PROFICIENT IN THOSE TWO STAGES WILL YOU BE READY FOR THE THIRD STAGE OF CHI SAO TRAINING. FOR NOW, BRUCE, THAT THIRD STAGE WILL REMAIN A SECRET FOR LATER. OKAY?

OKAY, MASTER!

WE WILL ALSO BE PRACTICING ON THIS KUNG FU WOODEN TRAINING DUMMY. SIMILARLY, BRUCE, THERE ARE STAGES AND MOVES TO PERFECT TO BECOME PROFICIENT WITH IT--108 MOVES, TO BE EXACT.

TO BEGIN, PRACTICE BLOCKING THE THREE WOODEN ARMS. FIRST ONE "ARM" AT A TIME . . .

. . . AND THEN PRACTICE A BLOCK OR TWO WITH A SINGLE COUNTERSTRIKE.

EVENTUALLY, YOU CAN PRACTICE MULTIPLE BLOCKS AND COUNTERS, AND ADD IN OBLIQUE KICKS TO THE DUMMY'S "LEG" TO GET USED TO YOUR FEET BEING PART OF YOUR COMBINATIONS.

THWACK THWACK THWACK THWACK THWACK THWACK THWACK THWACK THWACK

HOW CAN ANYONE MOVE THAT FAST?

145

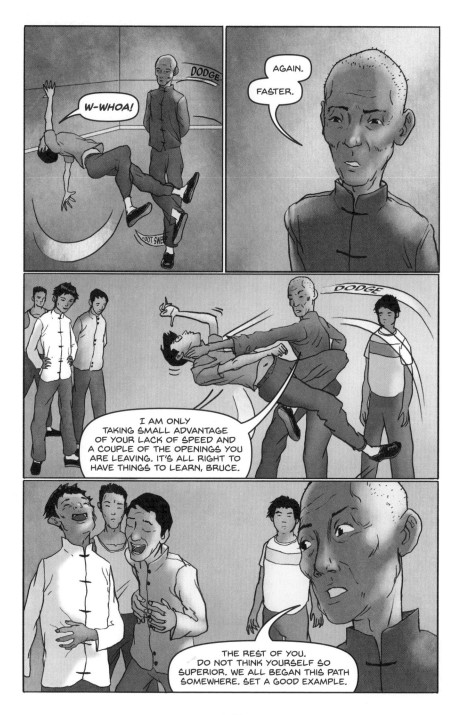

EVERYONE BACK TO TRAINING. I WILL COME AROUND AND WORK WITH YOU INDIVIDUALLY.

YES. THANK YOU FOR THE LESSON, MASTER.

BRUCE REMAINED TRUE TO HIS WORD TO RETURN TO THE KUNG FU STUDIO EVERY DAY AFTER SCHOOL.

HE HADN'T GOTTEN INTO TROUBLE IN WEEKS.

JUST AS WITH ACTING, KUNG FU WAS BRUCE'S NEW PASSION.

HURRY UP! THE MOB IS GONNA CATCH US!

AAAAAND CUT!

WHETHER ON THE SET OF A NEW MOVIE OR AT HOME IN HIS ROOM . . .

. . . HE WOULD PRACTICE HIS LINES *AND* THE NEW MOVES YIP MAN WAS WORKING ON WITH HIM.

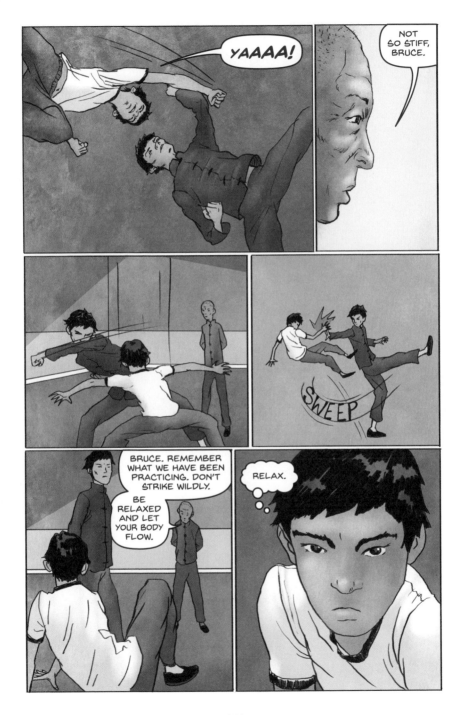

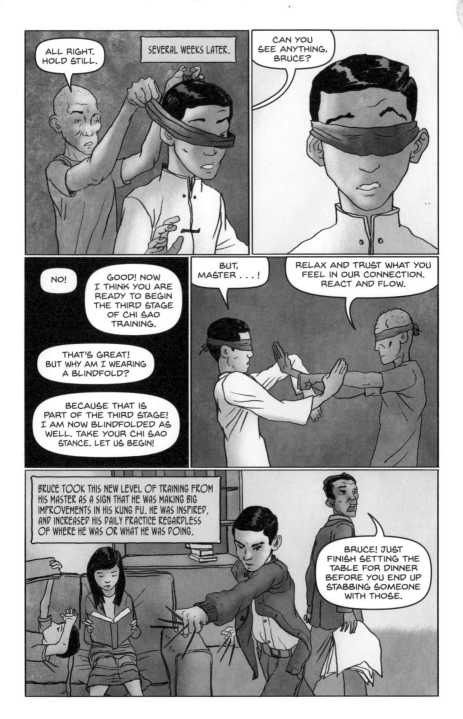

157

THE FOLLOWING WEEKS WERE A MIXTURE OF JOYFUL DANCING AND INNOCENT FLIRTATIONS AS BRUCE'S MANY YEARS OF DANCE PRACTICE WITH HIS SISTER WERE QUICKLY TAKEN TO THE NEXT LEVEL WITH HIS FREQUENT PRACTICES WITH AMY.

ALL THE WHILE, BRUCE'S SKILLS IN THE KUNG FU STUDIO HAD BEEN STEADILY INCREASING AS WELL.

ALL RIGHT, EVERYONE. PARTNER UP AND DO SOME RELAXED FREE FIGHTING FOR FIVE MINUTES.

161

163

CHAPTER 7

CHANGES AND DECISIONS

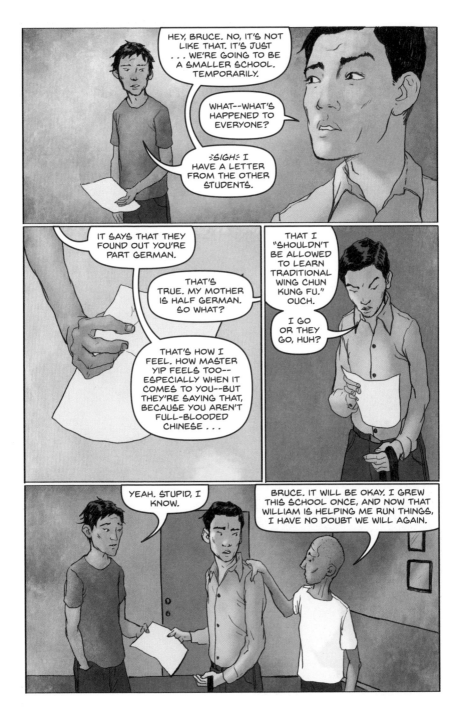

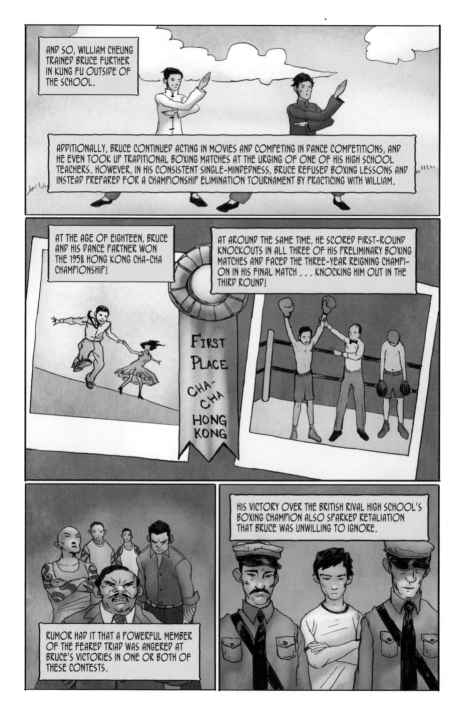

AND SO, WILLIAM CHEUNG TRAINED BRUCE FURTHER IN KUNG FU OUTSIDE OF THE SCHOOL.

ADDITIONALLY, BRUCE CONTINUED ACTING IN MOVIES AND COMPETING IN DANCE COMPETITIONS, AND HE EVEN TOOK UP TRADITIONAL BOXING MATCHES AT THE URGING OF ONE OF HIS HIGH SCHOOL TEACHERS. HOWEVER, IN HIS CONSISTENT SINGLE-MINDEDNESS, BRUCE REFUSED BOXING LESSONS AND INSTEAD PREPARED FOR A CHAMPIONSHIP ELIMINATION TOURNAMENT BY PRACTICING WITH WILLIAM.

AT THE AGE OF EIGHTEEN, BRUCE AND HIS DANCE PARTNER WON THE 1958 HONG KONG CHA-CHA CHAMPIONSHIP!

AT AROUND THE SAME TIME, HE SCORED FIRST-ROUND KNOCKOUTS IN ALL THREE OF HIS PRELIMINARY BOXING MATCHES AND FACED THE THREE-YEAR REIGNING CHAMPI-ON IN HIS FINAL MATCH . . . KNOCKING HIM OUT IN THE THIRD ROUND!

FIRST PLACE

CHA-CHA

HONG KONG

HIS VICTORY OVER THE BRITISH RIVAL HIGH SCHOOL'S BOXING CHAMPION ALSO SPARKED RETALIATION THAT BRUCE WAS UNWILLING TO IGNORE.

RUMOR HAD IT THAT A POWERFUL MEMBER OF THE FEARED TRIAD WAS ANGERED AT BRUCE'S VICTORIES IN ONE OR BOTH OF THESE CONTESTS.

171

CHAPTER 8

RETURN OF THE DRAGON

APRIL 1959.

WITH JUST $115 IN HIS POCKET, BRUCE BOARDED A SHIP BOUND FOR SAN FRANCISCO.

BRUCE WAS EIGHTEEN YEARS OLD AND DIDN'T KNOW A SOUL ON THE BOAT.

THREE WEEKS IN HERE??

. . . YOU USUALLY GET WHAT YOU PAY FOR.

THERE WAS ALSO THE FACT THAT HIS TICKET WAS QUITE CHEAP, AND . . .

WHAT A WASTE OF SUCH GOOD MUSIC!

THROUGH HIS CHARM, BRUCE MADE HIS WAY FROM HIS THIRD-CLASS PASSENGER QUARTERS INTO THE FIRST-CLASS SOCIAL AREA, ACTING AS THOUGH HE BELONGED THERE.

HE WATCHED THE WEALTHY PASSENGERS STAND IDLY BY WHILE SOME VERY GOOD MUSICIANS PLAYED DANCEABLE TUNES.

IN NO TIME, HE BEGAN SHOWING OFF HIS ABILITIES ON THE DANCE FLOOR AND SOON LED THE PASSENGERS IN A MASSIVE CHA-CHA LESSON THAT LASTED FOR HOURS!

FOR THE REST OF THE VOYAGE, BRUCE WAS WELCOME IN FIRST CLASS.

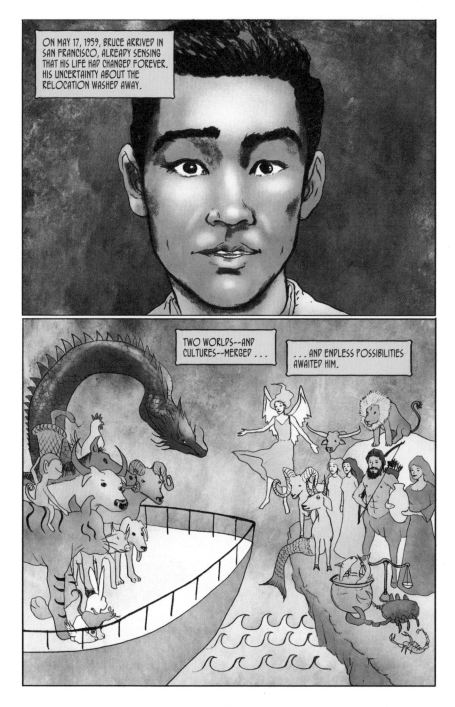

ON MAY 17, 1959, BRUCE ARRIVED IN SAN FRANCISCO, ALREADY SENSING THAT HIS LIFE HAD CHANGED FOREVER. HIS UNCERTAINTY ABOUT THE RELOCATION WASHED AWAY.

TWO WORLDS--AND CULTURES--MERGED . . .

. . . AND ENDLESS POSSIBILITIES AWAITED HIM.

BRUCE QUICKLY SETTLED INTO SEATTLE AND ENROLLED IN EDISON TECHNICAL SCHOOL TO COMPLETE HIS HIGH SCHOOL CREDITS AND GRADUATE.

IN MARCH 1961, HE ENROLLED AT THE UNIVERSITY OF WASHINGTON, WHERE HE WOULD MAJOR IN PHILOSOPHY. HE MARVELED WITH JOY AT THE SCHOOL'S EXTENSIVE LIBRARY.

HE TOOK FULL ADVANTAGE OF ITS WIDE VARIETY OF BOOKS.

TO SUPPORT HIMSELF, BRUCE TOOK ON MANY JOBS, INCLUDING STUFFING NEWSPAPERS AND WORKING EVENINGS AT RUBY CHOW'S RESTAURANT.

UNSURPRISINGLY, HE DID NOT LIKE TAKING ORDERS FROM CUSTOMERS.

ALL THE WHILE, BRUCE CONTINUED TO FIND TIME TO PRACTICE HIS KUNG FU AND TEACH A GROWING NUMBER OF STUDENTS.

UNFORTUNATELY, HIS KUNG FU "SCHOOL" WAS MERELY THE PARKING LOT OUTSIDE RUBY CHOW'S RESTAURANT, AND CLASSES HAD TO BE HELD AFTER HE FINISHED WAITING TABLES.

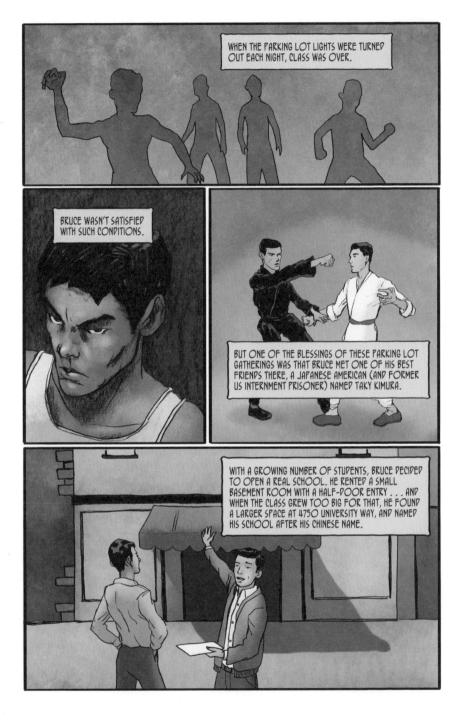

WHEN THE PARKING LOT LIGHTS WERE TURNED OUT EACH NIGHT, CLASS WAS OVER.

BRUCE WASN'T SATISFIED WITH SUCH CONDITIONS.

BUT ONE OF THE BLESSINGS OF THESE PARKING LOT GATHERINGS WAS THAT BRUCE MET ONE OF HIS BEST FRIENDS THERE, A JAPANESE AMERICAN (AND FORMER US INTERNMENT PRISONER) NAMED TAKY KIMURA.

WITH A GROWING NUMBER OF STUDENTS, BRUCE DECIDED TO OPEN A REAL SCHOOL. HE RENTED A SMALL BASEMENT ROOM WITH A HALF-DOOR ENTRY . . . AND WHEN THE CLASS GREW TOO BIG FOR THAT, HE FOUND A LARGER SPACE AT 4750 UNIVERSITY WAY, AND NAMED HIS SCHOOL AFTER HIS CHINESE NAME.

ON AUGUST 17, 1964, BRUCE AND LINDA GOT MARRIED.

OAKLAND, CALIFORNIA, USA

BRUCE LEFT CONTROL OF THE SEATTLE SCHOOL TO TAKY KIMURA, AND HE AND LINDA MOVED TO OAKLAND, CALIFORNIA.

HE RECONNECTED WITH HIS FRIEND JAMES LEE, AND THE TWO OF THEM OPENED BRUCE'S SECOND KUNG FU SCHOOL IN OAKLAND.

BRUCE AND LINDA WERE ENJOYING LIFE IN OAKLAND, AND BOTH SCHOOLS WERE FLOURISHING, UNTIL ONE DAY, WHEN BRUCE WAS TEACHING WHILE A MAN NAMED CLEAVON AND HIS SON LUCAS WERE OBSERVING THE CLASS . . .

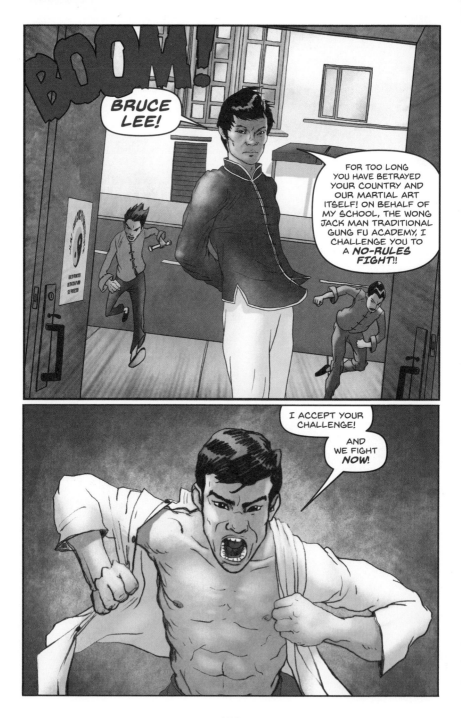

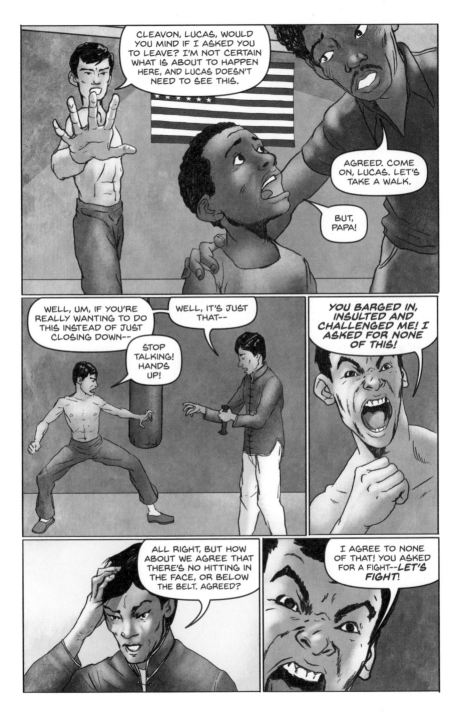

183

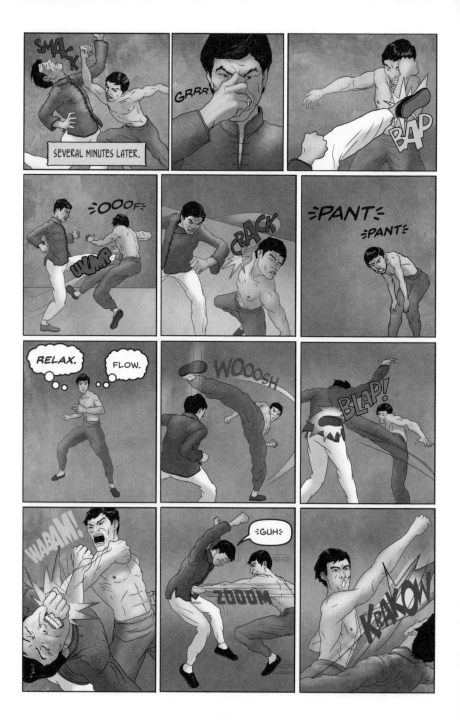

CHAPTER 9

JEET KUNE DO

192

BACK TRAINING, BRUCE ADDED WEIGHT LIFTING TO HIS REGIMEN AND INCREASED HIS TIME SPARRING.

JEEZ!

HE CAME UP WITH A NAME FOR HIS NEW FIGHTING STYLE: JEET KUNE DO (WHICH, TRANSLATED INTO ENGLISH, MEANS "WAY OF THE INTERCEPTING FIST").

NEXT TIME I'LL PUT A LIT MATCH IN MY TEETH FOR YOU TO BLOW OUT WITH YOUR KICK!

GREAT IDEA! I THINK I HAVE MATCHES IN MY DESK.

I WAS KIDDING, BRUCE.

YEP! TOP DRAWER. HEY, GET A CUP OF WATER READY IN CASE YOUR NOSE HAIR BURSTS INTO FLAMES--

KIDDING, BRUCE!

NOT GOING TO HAPPEN!

ALL RIGHT, ALL RIGHT. HEH. HEY, JAMES, WHAT'S THIS IN THE MAIL?

1ST ANNUAL INTERNATIONAL KARATE TOURNAMENT

IT WAS A LETTER INVITING BRUCE TO PUT ON A DEMONSTRATION OF HIS FIGHTING SKILLS AT THE FIRST INTERNATIONAL KARATE TOURNAMENT IN LONG BEACH, CALIFORNIA.

HIS RECENT ACQUAINTANCE, ED PARKER, WHO WAS KNOWN AS THE FATHER OF AMERICAN KENPO KARATE, WAS ORGANIZING THE EVENT.

BRUCE BROUGHT ALONG HIS FRIEND TAKY FROM SEATTLE TO HELP PUT ON HIS DEMONSTRATION.

BRUCE SHOWED SOME OF HIS TECHNIQUES AND CHARMED THE AUDIENCE WITH HIS HUMOR AND WEALTH OF MARTIAL-ARTS KNOWLEDGE.

WITH THE CROWD OF FELLOW FIGHTING-ARTS PRACTITIONERS, REPORTERS, AND PHOTOGRAPHERS UNDER HIS SPELL . . .

. . . HE WENT ON TO MESMERIZE THEM WITH HIS TWO-FINGERED PUSH-UPS.

AFTER EXPLAINING HOW MARTIAL ARTS CAN HARNESS POWER THAT MOST DON'T TAP INTO, EVEN AFTER YEARS OF TRAINING, BRUCE SPOKE OF A TECHNIQUE CALLED THE ONE-INCH PUNCH, WHICH WAS LITERALLY THAT. WITH MOSTLY DOUBTERS IN THE AUDIENCE, HE ASKED FOR A VOLUNTEER.

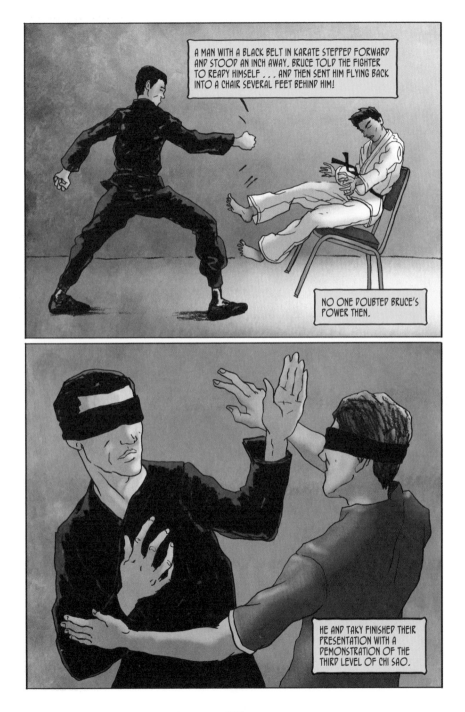

A MAN WITH A BLACK BELT IN KARATE STEPPED FORWARD AND STOOD AN INCH AWAY. BRUCE TOLD THE FIGHTER TO READY HIMSELF . . . AND THEN SENT HIM FLYING BACK INTO A CHAIR SEVERAL FEET BEHIND HIM!

NO ONE DOUBTED BRUCE'S POWER THEN.

HE AND TAKY FINISHED THEIR PRESENTATION WITH A DEMONSTRATION OF THE THIRD LEVEL OF CHI SAO.

BEFORE ANY HOLLYWOOD PATH COULD BEGIN, LIFE HAD OTHER PLANS. ON FEBRUARY 1, 1965, LINDA AND BRUCE WELCOMED THEIR SON, BRANDON, INTO THE WORLD. LIKE HIS FATHER, HE WAS BORN IN THE YEAR OF THE DRAGON!

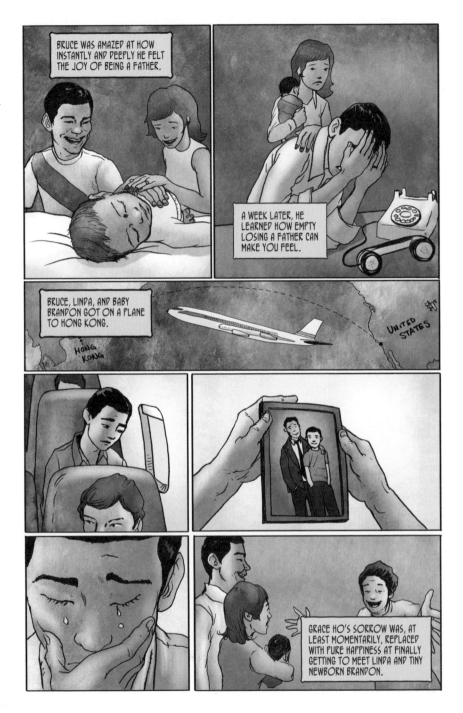

BRUCE WAS AMAZED AT HOW INSTANTLY AND DEEPLY HE FELT THE JOY OF BEING A FATHER.

A WEEK LATER, HE LEARNED HOW EMPTY LOSING A FATHER CAN MAKE YOU FEEL.

BRUCE, LINDA, AND BABY BRANDON GOT ON A PLANE TO HONG KONG.

HONG KONG

UNITED STATES

GRACE HO'S SORROW WAS, AT LEAST MOMENTARILY, REPLACED WITH PURE HAPPINESS AT FINALLY GETTING TO MEET LINDA AND TINY NEWBORN BRANDON.

DURING THEIR STAY IN HONG KONG, BRUCE GOT THE CHANCE TO CATCH UP WITH HIS MOTHER . . .

. . . INTRODUCE LINDA AND BRANDON TO HONG KONG . . .

. . . RECONNECT WITH HIS FAMILY . . .

. . . AND TRAIN ONCE AGAIN WITH YIP MAN.

THEY ENDED UP STAYING FOR FOUR MONTHS.

CHAPTER 10

HOLLYWOOD

UPON ARRIVING BACK IN THE UNITED STATES, BRUCE FOUND OUT THAT THE TELEVISION SHOW *THE GREEN HORNET* WAS GOING TO HAPPEN, WITH HIM AS ONE OF THE TWO LEAD ACTORS!

SEEING A FUTURE IN ACTING AND IN HOLLYWOOD, BRUCE, LINDA, AND BRANDON MOVED FROM OAKLAND TO LOS ANGELES IN MARCH OF 1966.

WITH TAKY KIMURA RUNNING THE KUNG FOO SCHOOL IN SEATTLE, BRUCE LEFT JAMES LEE IN CHARGE OF HIS OAKLAND SCHOOL.

COSTARRING AS KATO IN *THE GREEN HORNET* ALONGSIDE ACTOR VAN WILLIAMS, BRUCE WAS PAID $400 FOR EACH EPISODE. HE AND WILLIAMS PLAYED A CRIME-FIGHTING DUO WITH A BATMOBILE-TYPE CAR OF THEIR OWN, KNOWN AS THE BLACK BEAUTY.

THE SERIES FIRST AIRED ON SEPTEMBER 9, 1966. BRUCE INSISTED THAT HIS CHARACTER BE COOL AND INTIMIDATING RATHER THAN ADHERE TO THE ALL-TOO-OFTEN STEREOTYPED PORTRAYALS OF CHINESE CHARACTERS WHO USUALLY REPEATED LINES LIKE "AH, SO" AND "CHOP-CHOP."

BECAUSE OF HIS INSISTENCE, KATO WAS A FIRST GLIMPSE FOR MANY AMERICANS OF A CAPABLE CHINESE CHARACTER. IT WAS ALSO THEIR INTRODUCTION TO KUNG FU.

ALMOST IMMEDIATELY, BRUCE WAS TOLD TO SLOW DOWN HIS KICKS AND PUNCHES IN THE ACTION SCENES BECAUSE THEY WERE TOO QUICK FOR THE CAMERA TO CATCH. IT LOOKED LIKE HIS OPPONENTS WERE PASSING OUT AROUND HIM AS HE REMAINED STILL.

EVEN AFTER SLOWING DOWN, ONE REVIEW WROTE, BRUCE "STRIKES WITH SUCH SPEED THAT HE MAKES A RATTLER [SNAKE] LOOK LIKE A STUDY IN SLOW MOTION."

BRUCE, KATO, AND THE SHOW ALL MADE MANY FANS.

BRUCE WAS SCRATCHING THE SURFACE OF FAME IN AMERICA . . . AND HE ENJOYED IT!

THERE WAS EVEN A TWO-PART *GREEN HORNET* AND *BATMAN* CROSSOVER ON EACH OTHER'S SHOWS.

KAPOW!

WABANG!

THEN CAME A BIG SURPRISE. AFTER ONLY TWENTY-SIX EPISODES, THE SHOW WAS CANCELED!

CANCELED?!

WITH THE CANCELLATION, BRUCE AND LINDA NEEDED TO RELOCATE TO A PLACE THEY COULD BETTER AFFORD.

BRUCE NEEDED TO ACT QUICKLY TO BE ABLE TO SUPPORT HIS FAMILY. TEACHING KUNG FU WAS WHAT HE KNEW BEST.

HERE YOU ARE, MY FRIEND. IT'S A GREAT LOCATION.

BRUCE, ED PARKER, AND THEIR FRIEND AND ACCOMPLISHED MARTIAL ARTIST DAN INOSANTO WENT LOOKING FOR A LOCATION OF WHAT WOULD BECOME BRUCE'S THIRD SCHOOL, NOW IN LOS ANGELES.

WHAT DO YOU THINK?

LET'S GET THE REALTOR OUT HERE SO I CAN PUNCH AND KICK AROUND IN THERE FOR A FEW MINUTES TO GET A FEEL FOR THE SPACE.

BRUCE LIKED THE SPACE AND OPENED THE LOS ANGELES SCHOOL.

KNOWING THAT HE WANTED TO SPLIT HIS TIME BETWEEN TEACHING AND ACTING, HE BROUGHT DAN IN AS HIS CO-INSTRUCTOR, WHILE ALSO TRAINING DAN IN THE PRINCIPLES OF JEET KUNE DO.

HE ALSO BEGAN TEACHING PRIVATE LESSONS, OFTEN TO HOLLYWOOD INSIDERS, IN HIS BACKYARD.

ONE OF HIS STUDENTS, CHARLES FITZSIMONS, WHO'D BEEN AN ASSISTANT PRODUCER ON *THE GREEN HORNET*, MADE A BOLD SUGGESTION.

BRUCE, YOU KNOW AS WELL AS I DO THAT THERE'S MONEY TO BE HAD WITH US HOLLYWOOD TYPES.

RIGHT NOW YOU'RE CHARGING STUDENTS AT YOUR SCHOOL TWENTY-TWO DOLLARS A MONTH, BUT JUST A BIT MORE FOR THESE LESSONS.

WHAT I'M SAYING IS THAT YOU COULD CHARGE, SAY, FIFTY DOLLARS *AN HOUR* FOR THIS KIND OF PRIVATE INSTRUCTION.

WHAT? THAT'S JUST CRAZY.

BRUCE, THESE PEOPLE--MYSELF INCLUDED-- WE HAVE THE MONEY, AND WHAT YOU'RE TEACHING IS UNLIKE ANYTHING I'VE EVER HEARD OF OR SEEN HERE!

THE HIGHER RATES FROM THE WEALTHIER CLIENTS ENABLED BRUCE TO TEACH OTHERS AT HIS SCHOOL WHO DESPERATELY WANTED TO TRAIN BUT DIDN'T HAVE THE MONEY TO AFFORD MEMBERSHIP. IF A PERSON WAS COMMITTED ENOUGH TO LEARNING, BRUCE HAD NO PROBLEM TEACHING FOR FREE.

IN ADDITION TO TEACHING, BRUCE KEPT ACTING IN MOVIES AND TV SHOWS ALONGSIDE BIG STARS LIKE JAMES GARNER, TAKING SUPPORTING ROLES LIKE THIS ONE IN THE MOVIE *MARLOWE*, IN WHICH BRUCE PORTRAYED A VILLAIN!

HE ALSO HAD ROLES IN TV SHOWS LIKE *BLONDIE*, AND THIS ONE IN *IRONSIDE*, IN WHICH HE GOT TO ACT AND STUNT-FIGHT ALONGSIDE JUDO LEGEND "JUDO" GENE LEBELL (ALSO KNOWN AS "THE GODFATHER OF GRAPPLING"). THEY BECAME FRIENDS, AND BRUCE WOULD LATER CREDIT GENE WITH INSPIRING SOME OF THE GRAPPLING PRINCIPLES OF JEET KUNE DO.

THOUGH HE HAD NOT LANDED ANOTHER LEADING ROLE IN A TV SHOW OR MOVIE, BRUCE'S REPUTATION AS A MARTIAL ARTIST AND INSTRUCTOR WAS GROWING IN HOLLYWOOD.

AT ONE POINT, BRUCE WAS TEACHING PRIVATE LESSONS TO SOME OF THE BIGGEST NAMES IN MOVIES--STEVE MCQUEEN, JAMES GARNER, AND JAMES COBURN TO NAME A FEW.

MEANWHILE, BRUCE AND LINDA WERE EXPECTING A NEW ARRIVAL.

SHANNON LEE WAS BORN ON APRIL 19, 1969, DURING THE YEAR OF THE ROOSTER.

ONE MORNING SEVERAL MONTHS LATER, WITHOUT WARMING UP AS HE USUALLY DID, BRUCE LIFTED A HEAVY AMOUNT OF WEIGHTS UP ABOVE HIS HEAD.

IMMEDIATELY, HE WAS IN SUCH SEVERE BACK PAIN THAT HE WAS SOON IN THE HOSPITAL.

I FEAR THAT THERE IS NERVE DAMAGE TO YOUR SPINE AND LEGS.

YOU WILL NEED TO STAY IN BED FOR MONTHS TO RECOVER.

YOU MIGHT EVENTUALLY BECOME PAIN FREE--OR CLOSE TO IT--DURING NORMAL DAILY ACTIVITY LEVELS . . .

. . . BUT I'M AFRAID YOUR LIFE AS A MARTIAL ARTIST IS OVER. I CAN'T IMAGINE YOU WILL EVER BE ABLE TO KICK AGAIN.

NO OFFENSE, DOCTOR, BUT THERE IS NO WAY YOU'RE RIGHT ABOUT THAT!

DESPITE HIS STUBBORN DETERMINATION, BRUCE STILL NEEDED TIME FOR HIS INJURY TO HEAL.

HE RETURNED TO HIS STUDY OF THE MARTIAL ARTS THROUGH BOOKS. DURING HIS THREE-MONTH BED REST, HE WROTE WHAT WOULD LATER BE PUBLISHED IN BOOK FORM AS *THE TAO OF JEET KUNE DO.*

HE TRIED TO RECOVER FROM THE LOSS OF MUSCLE THAT HAD OCCURRED. THIS MEANT PAINSTAKINGLY SLOW WALKING . . .

. . . AND EVENTUALLY SOME MILD STRETCHING AND BODY-WEIGHT STRENGTH TRAINING.

FINALLY, AFTER MONTHS OF SLOW IMPROVEMENTS AND CAREFUL THERAPEUTIC EXERCISES, BRUCE OVERCAME HIS PROGNOSIS AND WAS ABLE TO KICK AGAIN!

THOUGH HE REGAINED ALL OF HIS PRE-INJURY SKILLS --AND EVEN SURPASSED THEM--HE WOULD ALWAYS NEED TO TAKE EXTRA GOOD CARE OF HIS BACK FROM THEN ON BY STRETCHING BEFORE WORKING OUT, FOLLOWED BY ICING AFTERWARD, AS WELL AS GETTING MASSAGES AND TAKING PAIN RELIEVERS AS NEEDED.

ONCE BETTER, BRUCE AND BRANDON TRAVELED TO HONG KONG TO VISIT HIS MOTHER AND FAMILY.

UPON ARRIVAL, BRUCE WAS SURPRISED BY EVERYONE'S REACTION.

≈GASP!≈ KATO!!

HEY LOOK, EVERYONE! IT'S KATO!

OH WOW! KATO!

KATO!

BACK IN THE OLD NEIGHBORHOOD, A LONG-AGO ACQUAINTANCE CAME BY.

HI, BRUCE! REMEMBER ME?

WHAT? UNICORN CHAN?! IS THAT YOU?

AHA HA! MOM, THIS IS UNICORN CHAN! REMEMBER--SORRY, UNICORN--THE BOY WHO WAS LOCKED IN THE SCHOOL BATHROOM?

WHAT? OH, YES! OH, YOU TROUBLEMAKERS, YOU TWO!

HEY, KID! ARE YOU BRUCE'S SON? DOES HE HAVE SOME STORIES TO TELL YOU WHEN YOU'RE OLDER!

BRUCE, I GOTTA BE HONEST, I HEARD YOU WERE BACK VISITING, AND, WELL, I KNOW YOU ACTED HERE ALL THROUGH YOUR CHILDHOOD, BUT ONCE PEOPLE SAW THAT YOU WERE FAMOUS IN HOLLYWOOD, NOW THEY THINK OF YOU AS A SUPERSTAR!

ANYHOW, I WORK FOR A MOVIE PRODUCER OVER HERE NAMED RUN RUN SHAW, AND I THINK YOU TWO SHOULD MEET!

THE NEXT DAY, UNICORN INTRODUCED BRUCE TO MR. SHAW. WHILE THEY COULDN'T AGREE ON A PRICE TO DO A MOVIE TOGETHER, MEETING MR. SHAW'S STAFF, PARTICULARLY RAYMOND CHOW, WOULD PAY OFF LATER.

WHEN BRUCE RETURNED TO THE STATES, HE WORKED HARD TO GET A PITCH TOGETHER TO TAKE TO WARNER BROTHERS PICTURES.

BRUCE! *I LOVE IT!* AND SO DOES EVERYONE ELSE!

I'LL BE IN TOUCH!

THE PITCH WAS FOR A TV SERIES FEATURING AN EASTERN MONK (TO BE PLAYED BY BRUCE, OF COURSE!) WHO ROAMED THE COUNTRYSIDE AND HELPED PEOPLE WHO NEEDED PROBLEMS SOLVED--USUALLY WITH A MIXTURE OF PHILOSOPHY, SMARTS, AND MORE THAN A LITTLE KUNG FU.

STARRING IN HIS OWN TV SERIES THAT HE HAD CREATED FROM THE GROUND UP?

HE WAS OVER THE MOON!

A FEW DAYS LATER, AFTER THE STUDIO'S ACQUISITIONS MEETING . . .

I DON'T GET IT. HOW IS THAT ACCURATE OR BELIEVABLE?

WELL . . . THEY DECIDED TO GO AHEAD WITH MY IDEA, BUT THEY SAID CASTING AN ASIAN LEAD ACTOR WAS TOO RISKY.

WHAT?

SO THEY'RE GOING TO CAST AN AMERICAN ACTOR WHO LOOKS VAGUELY ASIAN.

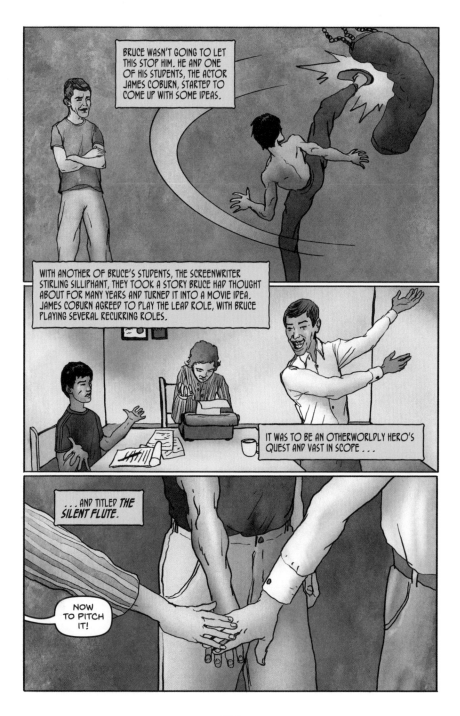

BRUCE WASN'T GOING TO LET THIS STOP HIM. HE AND ONE OF HIS STUDENTS, THE ACTOR JAMES COBURN, STARTED TO COME UP WITH SOME IDEAS.

WITH ANOTHER OF BRUCE'S STUDENTS, THE SCREENWRITER STIRLING SILLIPHANT, THEY TOOK A STORY BRUCE HAD THOUGHT ABOUT FOR MANY YEARS AND TURNED IT INTO A MOVIE IDEA. JAMES COBURN AGREED TO PLAY THE LEAD ROLE, WITH BRUCE PLAYING SEVERAL RECURRING ROLES.

IT WAS TO BE AN OTHERWORLDLY HERO'S QUEST AND VAST IN SCOPE . . .

. . . AND TITLED *THE SILENT FLUTE*.

NOW TO PITCH IT!

WHEN THEY GOT BACK HOME, THEY DISCOVERED THAT WARNER BROTHERS HAD CHANGED ITS MIND . . . AND JUST LIKE THAT--THE MOVIE WAS DEAD.

BUT BRUCE REFUSED TO LET DEFEAT BRING HIM DOWN.

THAT'S IT! EVERYONE, WE'RE GOING OUT FOR ICE CREAM!

WEEKS LATER.

THAT SOUNDS GREAT, MOM. I WILL SEE YOU SOON!

BRUCE TOOK A BRIEF TRIP BACK TO HONG KONG . . .

IN HONG KONG, BRUCE MET WITH RAYMOND CHOW, WHO HAD STARTED HIS OWN FILM COMPANY, GOLDEN HARVEST STUDIOS. THE TWO REACHED AN AGREEMENT TO DO TWO MOVIES TOGETHER . . . STARTING AS SOON AS POSSIBLE!

. . . THIS TIME TO HELP HIS MOTHER PREPARE TO MOVE TO THE UNITED STATES.

THE STUDIO PROVIDED AN APARTMENT IN HONG KONG FOR BRUCE AND HIS FAMILY WHILE THE MOVIES WERE BEING SHOT.

WU NGAN AND HIS WIFE ENDED UP MOVING IN WITH THE LEES FOR A SHORT TIME, AND BRANDON WAS OLD ENOUGH TO TEMPORARILY ATTEND BRUCE'S OLD MIDDLE SCHOOL, LA SALLE COLLEGE.

WITH GOLDEN HARVEST STUDIOS, BRUCE MADE TWO VERY SUCCESSFUL, ACTION-PACKED MOVIES.

THE BIG BOSS

THE PLOT OF THE MOVIE INVOLVES GANG MEMBERS FROM THAILAND THREATENING BRUCE AND OTHER CHINESE IMMIGRANTS LIVING IN BANGKOK. BRUCE'S CHARACTER TRIES TO REFRAIN FROM VIOLENCE BECAUSE OF A VOW HE MADE WITH HIS MOTHER (SIMILAR TO VOWS BRUCE HAD MADE IN HIS YOUTH). HOWEVER, HE IS DRAWN INTO HELPING HIS FRIENDS WHEN THEIR LIVES ARE ENDANGERED.

THE CHINESE CONNECTION
(AKA *FIST OF FURY*)

THIS MOVIE IS SET IN 1908 AND IS LOOSELY BASED ON HISTORICAL EVENTS. THE STORY REVOLVES AROUND BRUCE'S CHARACTER SEEKING REVENGE FOR THE DEATH OF HIS MARTIAL-ARTS TEACHER.

THE RELEASE OF **THE BIG BOSS** BROKE HONG KONG BOX OFFICE RECORDS . . . WHICH WERE THEN SHATTERED BY THE RELEASE OF **THE CHINESE CONNECTION!**

WITH PROOF OF HIS BANKABILITY, AS WELL AS REPEATED CLASHES WITH LO WEI, THE DIRECTOR OF BOTH MOVIES, BRUCE DECIDED TO ATTEMPT TO CREATE SOMETHING WHOLLY FROM HIMSELF ONCE AGAIN.

HE PLANNED TO WRITE, PRODUCE, DIRECT, CHOREOGRAPH, AND STAR IN IT. HE EVEN SCOUTED LOCATIONS AND HIRED ACTORS.

TWO SUCH ACTORS IN SMALL PARTS WOULD BE LONGTIME ACQUAINTANCE UNICORN CHAN, AS WELL AS WU NGAN.

BRUCE WANTED THE FIGHT SCENES TO BE REALISTIC, WHICH MEANT HE NEEDED A SKILLED AND FAST FOE. HE ENDED UP CASTING BOB WALL, AN AMERICAN KARATEKA AND A MUCH LARGER MAN THAN LEE. EVEN THOUGH THEY WERE GREAT ANTAGONISTS ON THE SCREEN, THEY BECAME GOOD FRIENDS OFF-SCREEN.

BRUCE CHOSE THE SIX-TIME US MIDDLEWEIGHT KARATE CHAMPION, CHUCK NORRIS, TO PLAY THE VILLAIN'S MOST DEADLY ENFORCER, COLT.

CASTING COMPLETE, BRUCE SHOT THE FILM, OVERSEEING ALL ASPECTS. HE EVEN ENDED UP PLAYING DRUMS ON THE MOVIE'S SOUNDTRACK. ONCE FINISHED, THE MOVIE WAS CALLED . . .

THE WAY OF THE DRAGON

THE FINAL BATTLE SCENE IS ONE OF THE MOST FAMOUS ON-SCREEN FIGHTS EVER, BUT MOST PEOPLE DON'T REALIZE THAT IT TOOK OVER FORTY-FIVE HOURS OF FILMING TO COMPLETE, AND WAS SHOT ILLEGALLY WITHIN ITALY'S ROMAN COLOSSEUM!

In *ENTER THE DRAGON*, BRUCE'S CHARACTER IS INVOLVED IN A DANGEROUS ELIMINATION-BOUT TOURNAMENT. BRUCE COWROTE, CODIRECTED, AND STARRED IN THE MOVIE, AND DECIDED TO HAVE FIGHT SCENES DEMONSTRATING A FEW OF THE JEET KUNE DO TECHNIQUES HE HAD DEVELOPED, WHICH INCLUDED GRAPPLING AND SUBMISSIONS, AN EVOLUTION FROM THE CHOREOGRAPHY OF HIS PREVIOUS MOVIES.

THE MOVIE WAS ONE OF THE BIGGEST BOX-OFFICE HITS OF THE YEAR AND IS STILL CONSIDERED TO BE ONE OF THE BEST MARTIAL-ARTS MOVIES EVER MADE.

BRUCE LEE'S PROSPECTS SEEMED LIMITLESS. BUT THEN, DURING THE FILMING OF THE MOVIE *GAME OF DEATH*, SOMETHING WENT HORRIBLY WRONG.

ON JULY 20, 1973, BRUCE LEE DIED IN HIS SLEEP AT THE AGE OF THIRTY-TWO, DUE TO AN ALLERGIC REACTION HE HAD TO SOME OVER-THE-COUNTER MEDICINE. WHAT WAS ONCE A BRIGHT FUTURE WAS CUT SHORT, AS THE FLAME OF LIFE WAS STOLEN FROM HIM.

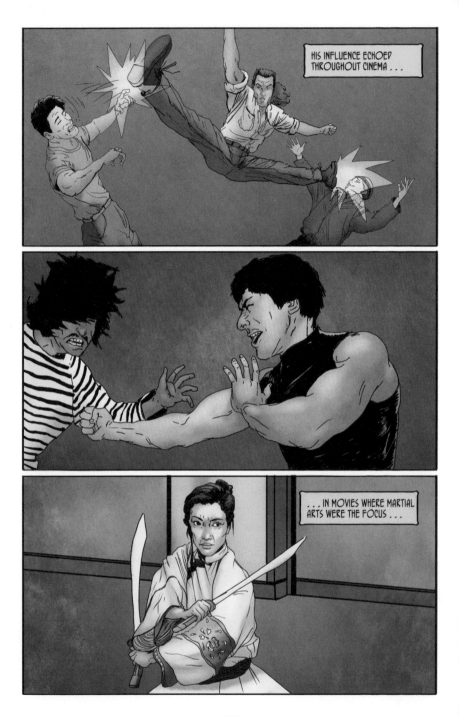

HIS INFLUENCE ECHOED THROUGHOUT CINEMA . . .

. . . IN MOVIES WHERE MARTIAL ARTS WERE THE FOCUS . . .

. . . AND IN MOVIES WHERE ACTORS ADMITTED CHANNELING BRUCE'S ATTITUDE IN THEIR MINDS WHEN CARRYING OUT A ROLE.

TO BE SURE, HIS THIRST FOR KNOWLEDGE AND IMPROVEMENT IS MOTIVATING CURRENT AND FUTURE MARTIAL ARTISTS TO THIS DAY.

"THE KEY TO IMMORTALITY IS FIRST LIVING A LIFE WORTH REMEMBERING."
-- BRUCE LEE

1971–Bruce with Brandon and Shannon

AUTHOR'S NOTE

In elementary school there wasn't much for me to do at home after homework and chores. One thing I always looked forward to was Black Belt Theater on Saturdays. The crazy awesome fight scenes had martial artists battling out their vengeance using flashy kicks and scary-sharp weapons. The heroes were always outnumbered and often died in the climax. I loved it.

You can imagine my thrill when I discovered Bruce Lee's movies—with his magnetic charm and the better plots and acting—just as I was finishing eighth grade and starting to train at a local Shotokan Karate dojo (school). My instant obsession with Bruce Lee and real-life love of martial arts collided and took off!

Fast-forward through college, the dojo closing, and becoming a husband, father, and artist. As an artist also wanting to write books, I kept returning to the idea of telling Bruce Lee's life story in a way that hadn't been done before, focusing largely on his childhood. I never aimed for it be a perfectly accurate, definitive take. With conflicting accounts and areas of thin information, there was a hazy fog over what might be the truth. But after reading books by and about him, the basic framework came clear and provided a structure upon which to build. Where facts are solid, I've related them truthfully. Where the unknown intervenes, I've imagined his childhood as it might have been. I've added fantastical zodiac elements, glossed over some of the specific violence in Bruce's youthful gang life, and depicted supporting characters in a fictional light. Even with these changes I hope I have remained respectful to the public image of Bruce Lee and to his family, both deceased and alive.

Bruce Lee was a complicated man, but I'm certain he was also a good man. He was a whirlwind of bravado and performance artist, but he also embodied the humility of a true martial artist and the mind of a philosopher. He mastered the body's capacity for violence, and was open to incorporating new skills from others. He also read and wrote often. He seemed to think that not only should the body be strong, but the mind as well, and he kept his mind sharp, and ever-curious. His writings and quotes that are catalogued in books and online are powerful, wise, thoughtful, meaningful, and unique—just like the man himself. I hope here to not only honor Bruce Lee, but also to introduce him to the young people of today and beyond. His pursuit of physical and mental improvement—as well as his outlook that all of us, while different, are interconnected as "one family"—is a timeless, positive philosophy that we could all do well to embrace.

I hope you have enjoyed my take on him and his legendary life and career.

Gratefully yours,

Jim Di Bartolo

ACKNOWLEDGMENTS

To my editor and friend, the masterful and prolific David Levithan, who saw the possibilities of a gem buried somewhere within my book dummy, and deftly guided me to create this book. David, you're an immense talent, and I hope I unearthed a good portion of the gem.

To Phil Falco, art director extraordinaire, for his vast knowledge of all things bookmaking-related. And thanks to the radly-skilled Shivana Sookdeo for doing countless things for this book. Special thanks to David Saylor and everyone at Graphix and Scholastic for all you do every day for this and so many other books.

To Kevin Tsang for giving me confidence in early drafts and for your willingness to read it in a messy book-dummy state.

Many thanks to Matt Wong, who stepped in to help Scholastic and myself be more certain that what I was creating was accurate where I wanted it to be, and sensitive where I had taken liberties in my storytelling.

To Guy Major and his truly gifted artistic eye, thank you for so skillfully seeing what I was doing on my colored pages and then so deftly replicating it throughout the book with exceptional elegance.

Unending thanks to my agent, Jane Putch, for rock-solid support, enthusiasm for wherever my creative interests wander, and for being such a dear friend.

To my mother, Sharon, and my late father, Jim, may he rest in peace. Thanks for all of your love and support of me as a child and into adulthood—I love you both so much!

To Jim and Patti Taylor, thank you for welcoming me into your family and for creating such a treat of a person in Laini. I am eternally grateful to you for that and more.

To Senseis Lamont, Bailey, Fischer, and Gasparakis: Thank you for your guidance, instruction, and inspiration, as well as lessons on discipline and tradition. Oss!

Thank you to librarians, teachers, and booksellers who "got it" about graphic novels well before much of the rest of the adult public.

To my daughter, Clementine, whose joy and silliness knows no bounds. May the world someday bend to your unwavering sense of justice, goodness, and inclusion. You had it all figured out years ago: be kind, share your toys, and play until you drop. I couldn't be more proud of the loving, creative, talented person your mother and I are raising, and I learn from you every day. I love you endlessly.

Lastly, to my wife, Laini. You and Clementine are my world. Thank you for giving me a ride back from art school way back when. Thank you for inviting me to your Halloween party. Thank you for saying yes when I proposed on a wobbling gondola in Venice a couple years later. Thank you for making me want to be a better artist, person, and parent, and for showing me the way through example. I love you infinitely.